Tech for Seniors

Essential Apps and Websites for a Digital Lifestyle

A Practical Guide to Navigating the Digital World with Confidence

By Oluchi Ike

Preface

In today's fast-paced, tech-driven world, staying connected and informed is more important than ever—no matter your age. Yet for many seniors, using smartphones, tablets, and websites can feel overwhelming. This book was created to break down those digital walls and empower older adults to confidently use technology in their everyday lives.

Whether you're looking to video chat with loved ones, keep track of your health, manage your finances, or simply explore the world from your screen, this guide walks you through it all—one easy step at a time. With clear instructions, real-life examples, and helpful tips, **Tech for Seniors** is your companion to making technology work *for you.*

Welcome to your digital lifestyle—made simple, secure, and enriching.

Table of Contents

Introduction

- Why Technology Matters at Every Age

- Benefits of Being Digitally Connected

- Common Barriers (and How to Overcome Them)

- Safety and Privacy First

Chapter 1: Getting Started with Smart Devices

1.1 Choosing the Right Device (Smartphones, Tablets, Laptops)

1.2 Setting Up Your Device Step-by-Step

1.3 Connecting to Wi-Fi

1.4 Adjusting Accessibility Settings (Text Size, Voice Commands, etc.)

Chapter 2: Mastering Communication Apps

2.1 Using Phone Calls and Text Messaging

2.2 Video Calling with Zoom, FaceTime, and Google Meet

2.3 Instant Messaging: WhatsApp, Messenger, and Telegram

2.4 Setting Up Email Accounts and Managing Messages

Chapter 3: Navigating Social Media

3.1 Introduction to Facebook, Instagram, and X (Twitter)

3.2 Creating and Managing Profiles

3.3 Sharing Photos, Comments, and Status Updates

3.4 Understanding Privacy Settings and Avoiding Scams

Chapter 4: Staying Informed Online

4.1 Finding Credible News Sources

4.2 Using News Aggregator Apps (Google News, Flipboard)

4.3 Watching News on YouTube and TV Apps

4.4 Avoiding Misinformation and Fake News

Chapter 5: Online Banking & Money Management

5.1 Using Online Banking Safely

5.2 Paying Bills and Transferring Money

5.3 Budgeting and Expense Tracker Apps

5.4 Shopping Online with Confidence

Chapter 6: Health and Wellness Apps

6.1 Using Fitness Trackers and Step Counters

6.2 Medication Reminder and Management Apps

6.3 Telehealth and Virtual Doctor Visits

6.4 Mental Wellness and Meditation Apps

Chapter 7: Organizing Daily Life with Apps

7.1 Calendar and Reminder Tools

7.2 Grocery and To-Do List Apps

7.3 Notes and Voice Memo Tools

7.4 Meal Planning and Recipe Apps

Chapter 8: Exploring Entertainment and Hobbies

8.1 Watching Movies and Shows (Netflix, Prime Video, YouTube)

8.2 Listening to Music and Podcasts

8.3 Playing Games for Brain Health

8.4 Joining Online Groups and Hobby Forums

Chapter 9: Learning New Skills Online

9.1 Using YouTube for Tutorials

9.2 Free Learning Platforms (Coursera, Khan Academy, Duolingo)

9.3 Virtual Libraries and eBooks

9.4 Lifelong Learning Communities for Seniors

Chapter 10: Digital Safety and Security

10.1 Creating Strong Passwords

10.2 Avoiding Online Scams and Phishing

10.3 Managing Privacy Settings on Apps and Websites

10.4 Backing Up Important Information

Chapter 11: Staying Connected with Family

11.1 Sharing Photo Albums and Memories

11.2 Using Family Apps (Life360, Shared Calendars)

11.3 Grandparent-Grandchild Tech Activities

11.4 Hosting Virtual Family Events

Chapter 12: Troubleshooting and Finding Help

12.1 Common Tech Problems and Fixes

12.2 Using Google and YouTube to Find Solutions

12.3 Getting Help from Trusted Tech Support

12.4 Local Tech Classes and Online Communities for Seniors

Conclusion

- Embracing the Digital World at Your Own Pace

- Encouragement for Continued Exploration

- You're More Tech-Savvy Than You Think!

- Final Tips and Next Steps

Author's Note

References

Introduction

Why Technology Matters at Every Age

In a world where everything from banking to birthday greetings happens online, technology has become more than a convenience—it's a lifeline. For older adults, staying connected through digital tools isn't just about being trendy; it's about staying *relevant, engaged,* and *empowered.* Whether it's catching up with distant family, checking in with your doctor from home, or reading the daily news on a tablet, technology provides an unprecedented level of accessibility and independence.

Some people assume technology is only for younger generations. But that couldn't be further from the truth. Seniors across the globe are embracing smartphones, tablets, and websites to make their lives easier, more enjoyable, and more connected. The goal of this book is to help you join that movement—comfortably and confidently.

You don't have to be a tech expert to reap the benefits of today's digital tools. What matters most is *willingness, curiosity,* and a little guidance—and that's exactly what this guide is here to provide.

Benefits of Being Digitally Connected

The digital world offers numerous advantages for seniors, many of which directly enhance daily living and overall well-being.

1. Staying Connected with Family and Friends

Social connection is a key contributor to mental and emotional health. Apps like WhatsApp, Zoom, and Facebook make it easier than ever to talk, video chat, or share photos with loved ones near and far. For grandparents especially, these tools can provide a front-row seat to the lives of children and grandchildren—no matter the distance.

2. Access to Health and Wellness Tools

Technology has revolutionized the way we manage our health. From medication reminders to virtual doctor visits, digital health apps help seniors track their wellness without leaving home. Wearables like step counters and smartwatches can encourage physical activity and even alert caregivers in case of a fall or emergency.

3. Lifelong Learning and Entertainment

With access to eBooks, educational videos, online classes, games, and hobby forums, technology opens the door to endless mental stimulation. Whether you want to learn a new language or watch your favorite classic movie, the internet puts a world of enrichment at your fingertips.

4. Convenience in Everyday Tasks

Online banking, grocery shopping, and appointment scheduling are just a few of the everyday tasks that can be simplified through apps and websites. This can be especially helpful for seniors with limited mobility or those living in remote areas.

5. Increased Independence

Digital tools support seniors in living more independently for longer. Managing your own finances, setting reminders for medications, or even navigating with GPS while driving—technology can be a powerful ally in preserving your freedom and autonomy.

Common Barriers (and How to Overcome Them)

While the benefits are clear, it's also important to acknowledge that getting started with technology isn't always easy. Many seniors face obstacles such as unfamiliarity, fear of making mistakes, or concerns about security. These are perfectly normal, but they're also surmountable.

1. Fear of the Unknown

Trying something new can be intimidating. Many older adults worry that they'll "break" something or press the wrong button. The truth is, most devices are designed to be user-friendly and offer undo options for mistakes. With some gentle exploration and practice, comfort grows over time.

Tip: Start small. Choose one app or tool you're genuinely interested in and learn just that. Once you gain confidence, the rest will follow naturally.

2. Lack of Confidence or Guidance

Without someone to show you the ropes, technology can feel like a foreign language. That's where books like this one come in. Step-by-step instructions and real-life examples can fill the gap when a tech-savvy grandchild isn't nearby.

Tip: Seek out senior-friendly tutorials online or ask a family member to show you the basics. Some communities even offer tech help classes specifically for older adults.

3. Physical Challenges

Arthritis, vision impairment, or hearing loss can make using devices more difficult. Thankfully, most smartphones and tablets include *accessibility features* like voice commands, larger text, and sound amplifiers.

Tip: Explore your device's settings under "Accessibility." You can customize almost everything—making your screen brighter, increasing text size, or enabling voice typing.

4. Feeling Left Behind

It's easy to feel like the world is moving too fast, but remember: *you don't have to know everything*. You only need to know what matters to *you*. Whether that's chatting with family, managing your medications, or watching the news—your digital lifestyle can be as simple or robust as you want it to be.

Safety and Privacy First

Before diving into apps and websites, it's important to set the stage with safety. Just like in the physical world, the digital space has both wonderful and risky areas. Learning how to navigate safely is a key part of building digital confidence.

1. Protecting Personal Information

Never share sensitive details—like Social Security numbers or banking information—unless you are 100% sure of who you're dealing with. Reputable apps and websites use encryption and secure sign-ins, but always double-check URLs and sources.

Tip: Look for "https://" in the web address and a small padlock symbol next to it—these indicate a secure site.

2. Creating Strong Passwords

Use strong, unique passwords for each account. Avoid easy-to-guess ones like "123456" or your birthday. Consider using a *password manager* app to help remember and organize them.

3. Recognizing Scams and Phishing

Emails or texts claiming "urgent action required" or promising a prize often aim to trick you into sharing personal data. Be cautious of unsolicited messages and links.

Tip: If something seems suspicious, delete it or ask a trusted person for a second opinion before clicking.

4. Keeping Devices Updated

Software updates often include important security patches. Make it a habit to install updates when prompted, and regularly check your device settings for any pending ones.

In Closing...

Technology is a tool—a bridge to connection, learning, and independence. It's never too late to begin your digital journey. This book will walk with you, step by step, making sure you feel secure and supported as you explore the online world. With patience and curiosity, the digital age can be your best age yet.

Chapter 1: Getting Started with Smart Devices

Technology might seem like a whole new world—but it's a world you *can* explore, one step at a time. At the heart of this digital journey are smart devices: tools that can help you communicate, learn, manage your health, and even shop from the comfort of your chair. This chapter will walk you through the basics of choosing, setting up, and customizing a device that suits your needs.

1.1 Choosing the Right Device (Smartphones, Tablets, Laptops)

Before jumping into the digital world, you need the right tool. There are three main types of smart devices to consider:

Smartphones

Smartphones are powerful handheld devices that combine the functions of a phone, camera, and computer. With a smartphone, you can make calls, send texts, use apps, take photos, and browse the internet.

- **Best for:** Calling, texting, health apps, navigation, and social media.

- **Popular options:** Apple iPhones (iOS) and Samsung or Google Pixel phones (Android).

Tablets

Tablets are larger than smartphones but smaller than laptops. They have touchscreens, are lightweight, and are great for reading, watching videos, browsing, and playing games. Many seniors enjoy tablets because they offer a bigger screen and easy-to-use apps.

- **Best for:** Reading, video calls, games, watching shows, and browsing.

- **Popular options:** iPad (iOS), Samsung Galaxy Tab (Android), Amazon Fire tablet.

Laptops

Laptops offer a full keyboard and larger screen, making them ideal for longer tasks like typing documents, managing email, or online banking. They're not as portable as smartphones or tablets, but they're more powerful.

- **Best for:** Writing emails, online classes, web browsing, banking, and photo storage.

- **Popular options:** MacBook (Apple), Dell, HP, Lenovo (Windows), and Chromebooks.

How to Choose

- **For simplicity:** Go with a tablet or smartphone.

- **For larger text and screens:** Choose a tablet or laptop.

- **For traditional typing:** A laptop is your friend.

- **For a mix of everything in your pocket:** Smartphones are compact and versatile.

Remember, there's no right or wrong choice—only what fits your *comfort*, *needs*, and *budget*.

1.2 Setting Up Your Device Step-by-Step

Once you've picked your device, it's time to get started. Don't worry—it's easier than you think!

Step 1: Turn it on

Press and hold the power button (usually on the side or top of the device) until the screen lights up.

Step 2: Choose your language and region

You'll be asked to select your preferred language (e.g., English) and country.

Step 3: Connect to Wi-Fi *(More on this in the next section.)*

Wi-Fi allows your device to access the internet. You'll need to select your home Wi-Fi name and enter the password.

Step 4: Sign in or create an account

You'll be asked to sign in using an Apple ID (for iPhones/iPads) or a Google account (for Android devices and Chromebooks). These accounts store your preferences, download apps, and sync data.

- **Apple users**: Create an Apple ID.

- **Android/Chromebook users**: Use or create a Google (Gmail) account.

If you're unsure how to set one up, ask a family member or follow the on-screen steps.

Step 5: Enable updates

Your device may download updates to improve performance and security. It's okay to allow this—it's a good thing!

Step 6: Set a passcode or fingerprint

For security, your device will ask if you want to set a password, PIN, or fingerprint. Choose one that's easy to remember but not easy for strangers to guess.

Step 7: Explore your home screen

Once set up, you'll see a "home screen" with icons for apps like Phone, Messages, Camera, and Settings.

That's it! You're ready to begin using your device.

1.3 Connecting to Wi-Fi

Wi-Fi is like your device's gateway to the internet. Without it, you can still use your phone or tablet, but you won't be able to browse websites, check email, or use most apps.

How to Connect to Wi-Fi:

1. **Open Settings**

   Look for the gear icon ⚙☐ labeled "Settings" on your home screen.

2. **Select "Wi-Fi" or "Network & Internet"**

   This will show available networks.

3. **Choose Your Network Name**

   This is usually written on a sticker on your router or provided by your internet service provider.

4. **Enter the Password**

   Be careful with capital letters and symbols.

5. **Tap Connect or Join**

Once you're connected, your device should automatically remember the Wi-Fi network for next time. You'll usually see a fan-shaped Wi-Fi symbol at the top of your screen when connected.

1.4 Adjusting Accessibility Settings (Text Size, Voice Commands, etc.)

To make your device easier to use, you can customize its settings. Modern devices include a range of *accessibility features*—perfect for anyone with visual, hearing, or dexterity challenges.

Increase Text Size

Reading tiny print? You can make it larger!

- **iPhone/iPad**:

   Go to *Settings → Display & Brightness → Text Size*

- **Android**:

   Go to *Settings → Display → Font size or Accessibility*

Slide the bar to increase or decrease text size. You can also enable **Bold Text** for extra clarity.

Enable Voice Commands (Voice Assistants)

Devices now let you speak instead of type!

- **iPhone/iPad**:

   Say "Hey Siri" to ask questions, set reminders, or send messages.

- **Android**:

  Say "Hey Google" or "OK Google" for similar tasks.

Example commands:

- "What's the weather today?"

- "Call Mary."

- "Set a reminder for my pills at 8 PM."

Color and Contrast Settings

If you're sensitive to bright light or need higher contrast:

- Enable *Dark Mode* to reduce glare.

- Increase contrast in the *Accessibility* menu.

🔊 Hearing Assistance

For those with hearing loss, devices support:

- **Closed captions** for videos.

- **Live transcription** (on newer phones).

- **Bluetooth hearing aid connections** for clearer sound.

Touch and Interaction Settings

If tapping small buttons is difficult:

- Use *Touch Accommodations* to adjust how the screen reacts.

- Enable *AssistiveTouch* (Apple) or *Accessibility Menu* (Android) to add large on-screen buttons.

Zoom or Magnifier Tools

Zoom into a portion of the screen using:

- *Zoom* (Apple)

- *Magnification Gestures* (Android)

You can even use your camera as a magnifier to read fine print in real life.

In Summary

Getting started with smart devices doesn't have to be overwhelming. The key is to start slow and choose a device that meets your needs and lifestyle. With the right setup and accessibility features, your smartphone, tablet, or laptop can become a reliable, user-friendly companion—whether you're video calling a grandchild, managing medications, or reading your favorite news site.

In the next chapter, we'll dive into **Essential Communication Apps**—including how to make video calls, send messages, and stay connected with loved ones near and far.

Chapter 2: Mastering Communication Apps

Communication is at the heart of staying connected—especially as the world becomes more digital. Whether it's calling a loved one, joining a family video chat, or sending a quick message, smart devices make it easier than ever. This chapter introduces the essential communication tools: phone calls, texts, video calls, messaging apps, and email. By the end, you'll be confidently chatting, texting, and connecting from anywhere.

2.1 Using Phone Calls and Text Messaging

Let's start with the basics—good old-fashioned phone calls and text messages, now done through smart devices.

Making a Phone Call

1. Tap the **Phone** icon (usually a green square with a white phone).

2. Select **Contacts** or use the **Keypad** to dial a number.

3. Tap the **Call** or **Green Phone** button.

4. To end the call, tap the **Red Phone** icon.

Tip: Save important numbers to your Contacts so you don't have to remember or retype them each time.

✉☐ Sending a Text Message

1. Tap the **Messages** app (green icon with a speech bubble on iPhone, or blue/white icon on Android).

2. Tap **New Message** or the **+** icon.

3. Type the contact's name or number.

4. Type your message and tap **Send** (usually a paper airplane or arrow icon).

Bonus Tips:

- You can attach **photos, emojis, or voice notes** to messages.

- Long-pressing a message lets you **react** with a thumbs-up or heart.

Texting is great for quick check-ins: *"How are you feeling today?"* or *"I'm on the way!"*

2.2 Video Calling with Zoom, FaceTime, and Google Meet

Seeing someone's face makes a big difference. Whether it's a birthday, a doctor's consult, or just saying hi to the grandkids, video calling makes it possible.

FaceTime (Apple Devices Only)

- Open the **FaceTime** app.

- Tap **New FaceTime** and choose a contact.

- Tap the **Video** icon to begin the call.

FaceTime only works between Apple devices (iPhone, iPad, Mac).

Google Meet

Great for Android users—or anyone with a Gmail account.

- Open the **Google Meet** app.

- Tap **New Meeting** to start a call or **Join with Code** if invited.

- Invite others by sharing the link or adding their Gmail.

Bonus: Google Meet works across devices (Android, Apple, computer).

Zoom

Perfect for group calls, classes, or virtual events.

1. **Download** the Zoom app.

2. Tap **Join Meeting** or **Sign Up** for an account.

3. Enter the **Meeting ID** and your **name**.

4. Tap **Join** and then **Connect Audio**.

Zoom offers **mute**, **camera on/off**, and **chat features**. It may take a little getting used to, but it's popular for a reason.

Video Call Tips for Success:

- Sit in a well-lit space.

- Look at the camera (near the top of the screen).

- Use headphones if the sound isn't clear.

- Tap the **mute/unmute** button if others can't hear you.

2.3 Instant Messaging: WhatsApp, Messenger, and Telegram

Instant messaging apps go beyond basic texts—they let you send photos, videos, voice notes, documents, and even make free calls over Wi-Fi.

WhatsApp

One of the most popular apps worldwide. Easy, secure, and free.

- **Download** WhatsApp from the App Store or Google Play.

- **Sign up** with your phone number.

- Add contacts who also use WhatsApp.

- Start a **chat**, send messages, photos, or tap the **phone** or **video** icon to call.

Why Seniors Love WhatsApp:

- Easy voice and video calls.

- Simple interface.

- Can create family groups to stay in touch with everyone at once.

💬 Facebook Messenger

If you use Facebook, Messenger lets you chat with your Facebook friends.

- **Open Messenger** (a separate app).

- Tap a person's name to start a chat.

- You can also **video call**, **send GIFs**, and **share location**.

You don't need to be friends with someone on Facebook to message them—but they may need to accept the message first.

Telegram

A safe, fast messaging app.

- Less cluttered than Messenger.

- Great for sharing larger files or joining interest-based groups (health tips, news, etc.).

All three apps work on **Wi-Fi** or mobile data—so you can stay in touch even without using your minutes.

2.4 Setting Up Email Accounts and Managing Messages

Email is still essential—especially for receiving updates from your doctor, bank, or favorite stores. Setting up an email account opens the door to newsletters, receipts, appointment reminders, and more.

How to Set Up an Email Account

Option 1: Create a Gmail account (Recommended)

1. Visit gmail.com or open the **Gmail** app.

2. Tap **Create Account** → For Myself.

3. Enter your name, choose a username (like mary.johnson82), and create a password.

4. Add a phone number and recovery email for security.

5. Agree to terms, and you're in!

Apple users may prefer an **iCloud** email: you can sign up during iPhone/iPad setup or in Settings > Mail.

Using the Email App

Once your account is ready, open the **Mail** or **Gmail** app to read, send, and manage your messages.

- **Inbox:** Where new emails land.

- **Sent:** Messages you've sent.

- **Spam:** Suspicious or unwanted messages.

To send an email:

1. Tap **Compose** or the **+** icon.

2. Enter the **email address** of the recipient.

3. Add a **subject line** (e.g., "Hello from Grandpa!").

4. Type your message.

5. Tap **Send** (paper airplane icon).

Email Tips:

- Be cautious of emails asking for personal information—especially from unknown senders.

- You can unsubscribe from marketing emails by clicking **Unsubscribe** at the bottom.

- Delete junk mail regularly to keep things tidy.

In Summary

Communication apps open the door to staying socially connected, emotionally supported, and mentally active. Whether you're sharing updates via text, seeing loved ones on video calls, or sending a cheerful email, the digital world makes it possible with just a tap or two.

There's no need to rush—practice each method at your own pace. Ask family or friends to walk you through it, or write down steps you find helpful. The more you use these tools, the more confident you'll become.

In the next chapter, we'll explore **Online Safety and Digital Scams**—how to protect your information, spot suspicious activity, and surf the web safely.

Chapter 3: Navigating Social Media

In today's world, social media is like a digital neighborhood—it's where people gather, share stories, connect with loved ones, and stay up to date on the world around them. For seniors, it offers a wonderful way to keep in touch with family, find old friends, explore hobbies, and feel part of a larger community—all from the comfort of home.

This chapter breaks down the basics of the three most popular platforms— **Facebook, Instagram,** and **X (formerly Twitter)**. We'll walk you through setting up profiles, posting photos, interacting with others, and most importantly, staying safe.

3.1 Introduction to Facebook, Instagram, and X (Twitter)

Let's begin by understanding what each platform is and what it's best used for:

Facebook

Facebook is like a digital living room. It allows you to:

- Connect with family and friends

- Share photos and updates

- Join groups based on hobbies or interests

- Follow local news, businesses, or religious communities

Most people start their social media journey with Facebook because it's user-friendly and offers a wide range of features in one place.

Instagram

Instagram is more visual—it's all about photos and videos. It's popular among younger generations, but seniors enjoy it too, especially for:

- Sharing travel pictures or garden updates

- Following grandchildren and seeing their stories

- Discovering beautiful content about food, art, or nature

You scroll through pictures and videos, often with short captions, making it simple and enjoyable.

X (Formerly Twitter)

X (Twitter) is a place for short messages, news, and quick thoughts.

- Good for following the latest headlines or trending topics

- Great for seeing quotes, jokes, or short tips

- Not focused on deep connections but excellent for staying informed

Each platform serves a purpose. You can use one, two, or all three depending on your comfort level and interests.

3.2 Creating and Managing Profiles

To use social media, you need a **profile**—your digital identity. Here's how to create and manage one on each platform:

Creating a Facebook Profile

1. Go to www.facebook.com or open the Facebook app.

2. Click or tap **Create New Account**.

3. Enter your name, email or phone, birthday, and a secure password.

4. Choose a **profile picture** (a nice photo of yourself).

5. Add information such as hometown, school, or work (optional).

Facebook will suggest people you might know—only accept friend requests from people you recognize.

Creating an Instagram Profile

1. Download the Instagram app.

2. Tap **Sign Up** and use your email or phone number.

3. Choose a **username** (e.g., NanaMary72) and password.

4. Add a profile picture and short bio like: *"Lover of plants, puzzles, and pie."*

Instagram will connect you to people from your phone contacts or Facebook if you allow it.

Creating an X (Twitter) Profile

1. Visit www.twitter.com or use the X app.

2. Tap **Sign Up**, enter your name, email or phone, and birthday.

3. Choose a unique **handle** (e.g., @GrandpaJoeSpeaks).

4. Upload a profile photo and write a short bio (e.g., "Retired teacher. Lifelong learner.").

With all profiles, it's a good idea to **write down your password** in a safe place and **turn on two-step verification** (extra layer of security).

3.3 Sharing Photos, Comments, and Status Updates

Once your profile is ready, it's time to engage with the world around you.

Sharing Photos

- On **Facebook or Instagram**, tap the **+** icon or "Photo" button.

- Choose a photo from your gallery or take a new one.

- Add a caption (optional), like: *"Beautiful morning walk in the garden."*

- Tap **Post** or **Share**.

This is a great way to share birthday pictures, family gatherings, or even just a blooming flower you're proud of.

Commenting and Liking

- When you see a post you enjoy, tap **Like** (a thumbs-up or heart icon).

- You can also tap **Comment** to leave a note like *"So proud of you!"* or *"Looks delicious!"*

This builds connection and shows your support. Don't worry about saying something "perfect"—your kind words mean a lot.

Posting a Status Update (Facebook)

1. Tap "What's on your mind?"

2. Type a message like *"Feeling thankful for good health today."*

3. Add emojis or tag a location if you'd like.

4. Tap **Post**.

You control who sees your posts—just friends, public, or private. We'll talk more about privacy in the next section.

3.4 Understanding Privacy Settings and Avoiding Scams

While social media is fun and enriching, it's important to use it wisely and protect yourself.

Understanding Privacy Settings

Each platform allows you to choose who can see your posts, send you messages, or find your profile.

- On **Facebook**, go to **Settings & Privacy > Privacy Checkup**. It walks you through:

  o Who can see your posts

  o Who can send you friend requests

  o What personal information is shared

- On **Instagram**, you can make your account **Private**, so only approved followers can see your content.

- On **X (Twitter)**, you can limit replies to only people you follow or turn your account private.

Golden Rule: Only connect with people you know and trust.

Avoiding Common Scams

Unfortunately, some people misuse social media to trick or scam others. Stay alert and remember:

- **Never share your Social Security number**, banking details, or passwords.

- Don't click links from strangers. These could be phishing scams trying to steal your data.

- Ignore messages that say you've won something—unless it's from a verified page.

- Be wary of messages that seem urgent or emotional (e.g., "I need money right now!"). Always call to verify if it's a real friend.

If anything seems suspicious:

- Report it using the platform's tools.

- Block the person.

- Ask a trusted family member or friend for a second opinion.

Enable Two-Factor Authentication on each account. This sends a text or email confirmation when someone logs in—it's an extra lock on your digital door.

In Summary

Social media can feel overwhelming at first, but like any new skill, it gets easier with practice. Start slow. Explore Facebook to catch up with family photos, use Instagram to admire beautiful images, or follow a few news sites on X to stay current.

Don't worry about being perfect—everyone starts somewhere. Ask loved ones to help you set up your profiles or walk you through posts. You'll find that social media can be a joyful, enriching way to stay connected, express yourself, and never feel left out of the conversation.

In the next chapter, we'll explore **Online Safety and Digital Scams** in greater depth—because staying connected also means staying protected.

Chapter 4: Staying Informed Online

In a world that changes by the minute, staying informed helps you make better decisions, engage in meaningful conversations, and feel more connected to what's happening in your community and around the globe. But with so much information floating around online, it's important to know **where to look**, **whom to trust**, and **how to spot misinformation**.

This chapter will walk you through how to find credible news sources, use apps that gather top stories for you, watch the news using modern streaming services, and—perhaps most importantly—how to **avoid fake news** and misleading headlines.

4.1 Finding Credible News Sources

Not all news sources are created equal. Some websites aim to inform, while others may be biased, sensational, or even completely false. Here's how to find **reliable, trustworthy news**:

Look for Established News Outlets

Well-known organizations have professional journalists and editors who follow ethical guidelines. These include:

- **BBC News** (bbc.com)

- **Reuters** (reuters.com)

- **Associated Press (AP)** (apnews.com)

- **NPR** (npr.org)

- **PBS NewsHour** (pbs.org)

- **Local newspapers** (like your city or state news station)

These sources typically provide balanced reporting and check their facts before publishing.

Look for Indicators of Credibility

When you're on a website or reading an article:

- **Check the date** – Is the information recent and still relevant?

- **Look for the author** – Are they a real journalist or expert? Click their name to see other articles they've written.

- **Check for sources** – Good reporting often links to documents, research, or official statements.

- **Avoid clickbait** – Headlines written to shock or scare ("You won't believe what happened!") are usually untrustworthy.

You can also use tools like **Media Bias/Fact Check** (mediabiasfactcheck.com) to check a site's political bias and reliability.

4.2 Using News Aggregator Apps (Google News, Flipboard)

If visiting multiple news websites feels like too much, consider using a **news aggregator app**—a tool that brings stories from many sources into one easy-to-read feed.

Google News

- **How to Access**: Visit news.google.com or download the **Google News app** on your phone.

- **How It Works**: Google News gathers stories from thousands of trusted sources and personalizes what you see based on your interests (politics, sports, health, etc.).

- You can follow topics (e.g., "COVID-19" or "Retirement"), local news, or even specific publications.

- Each article includes multiple viewpoints, so you can compare how different outlets are reporting the same story.

Flipboard

- **How to Access**: Download the **Flipboard app** or visit flipboard.com.

- **How It Works**: Flipboard turns news into a visual, magazine-style layout. You "flip" through articles by swiping, just like turning pages.

- You choose what you care about—like gardening, travel, health, or technology—and Flipboard curates those topics.

Both apps are free, easy to use, and designed to keep you informed without being overwhelming.

4.3 Watching News on YouTube and TV Apps

For many seniors, watching the news feels more natural than reading it. Thankfully, you can now access live or recorded news using your smart device, smart TV, or even your smartphone.

YouTube

- YouTube isn't just for music and comedy—it's also a great place to **watch the news**.

- Popular channels include:

  - **CBS News**

  - **NBC News**

  - **CNN**

  - **Sky News**

  - **Al Jazeera English**

- Simply go to youtube.com or open the app, then search for the name of the channel you want.

 Tip: Subscribe to your favorite news channels so you see updates on your home page.

TV Apps and Streaming Services

- Most major news stations have their own apps:

  - **CNN, Fox News, MSNBC, ABC News**, etc.

- If you have a **smart TV**, you can download these apps to watch live.

- Platforms like **Pluto TV** and **Roku Channel** also stream news 24/7 for free.

Voice Command Tip: If you're using a device like Amazon Fire TV or Google Assistant, just say, "Play the news," and it will load the latest headlines.

4.4 Avoiding Misinformation and Fake News

One of the biggest challenges of being online is **not everything you see is true**. Misinformation—intentionally or accidentally false information—can spread quickly and confuse even the most educated readers.

Here's how to protect yourself:

Spot the Warning Signs of Fake News

- **Sensational Headlines**: "Scientists say coffee will kill you!" (Really?)

- **Lack of Sources**: No links, references, or names of real people or organizations.

- **Errors and Poor Grammar**: Professional outlets rarely have sloppy writing.

- **Overuse of Capital Letters and !!!!!!!!!**: Designed to create panic or outrage.

Cross-Check with Trusted Outlets

If something sounds strange or too dramatic, check another reliable source to see if it's being reported elsewhere. For example, if a website claims a new health cure exists, but NPR or the CDC hasn't mentioned it, it may be false.

Use Fact-Checking Websites

When in doubt, check the story using one of these helpful tools:

- **Snopes.com**

- **PolitiFact.com**

- **FactCheck.org**

- **Hoax-Slayer.net**

These sites investigate rumors, viral posts, and misleading headlines.

💬 Don't Share Until You're Sure

Before forwarding a post or article to friends and family, take a moment to verify the information. Even well-meaning people can spread false info accidentally.

In Summary

Staying informed in the digital age can be empowering, fun, and incredibly useful—but only when you have the tools to do it right. With a few trustworthy apps and websites, a little curiosity, and the habit of checking your sources, you'll be more connected and better informed than ever before.

Remember:

- Choose **credible news outlets** like BBC, AP, or NPR.

- Use **news aggregator apps** like Google News or Flipboard to simplify your reading experience.

- **Watch news** through YouTube or TV apps if you prefer listening and watching over reading.

- Always **check facts**, **stay calm**, and **don't believe everything at first glance**.

You don't need to read the news all day—just a few minutes each morning or evening will help you stay sharp, safe, and engaged with the world around you.

 Up Next: In Chapter 5, we'll look at how to **manage your health digitally**, including using apps for medication tracking, doctor appointments, and wellness routines.

Chapter 5: Online Banking & Money Management

Managing money has come a long way from balancing checkbooks and visiting bank tellers. With today's technology, you can check your balance, pay bills, transfer money, and shop online—all from the comfort of your home. For seniors, online financial tools can provide **greater control**, **convenience**, and **peace of mind**. But it's important to learn how to use them **safely and smartly**.

This chapter will guide you through the essentials of online banking, paying bills, tracking your spending, and shopping online securely.

5.1 Using Online Banking Safely

Online banking lets you do almost everything you would at a physical bank branch—without waiting in line. Whether you use your bank's website or its mobile app, the first priority is **security**.

Setting Up Online Banking

1. **Visit Your Bank's Official Website** or download their app (e.g., Chase, Bank of America, Wells Fargo, etc.).

2. **Create a username and password.** Use a **strong password** that includes upper and lowercase letters, numbers, and symbols.

3. **Set up two-factor authentication (2FA)** if available. This adds an extra layer of protection by sending a code to your phone when you log in.

Tips for Safe Banking

- **Only log in on secure Wi-Fi** (avoid public networks at coffee shops).

- **Don't share your login credentials** with anyone—not even someone who says they're from your bank.

- **Sign out** of your account when finished, especially on shared devices.

- **Watch for phishing emails or texts** pretending to be from your bank. If you get a message that seems suspicious, contact your bank directly—don't click links.

Common Online Banking Features

- View checking/savings account balances.

- See recent transactions and deposits.

- Transfer money between your accounts.

- Set up account alerts for deposits or unusual activity.

5.2 Paying Bills and Transferring Money

Paying bills online is faster, easier, and helps avoid late fees. No need for envelopes, stamps, or trips to the post office.

How to Pay Bills Online

There are three main ways:

1. **Through Your Bank's Website or App**

   o Most banks let you **add payees** (like your electric company or internet provider).

- o You can schedule payments once or set up **automatic recurring payments**.

2. **Directly on a Company's Website**

   - o Utility providers, phone companies, and credit card issuers often have a **"Pay My Bill"** section on their websites.

   - o You can log in with your account number and use a debit card or bank transfer.

3. **Using Payment Services**

   - o Services like **PayPal**, **Venmo**, or **Zelle** let you pay individuals or companies quickly.

   - o These are useful for paying friends or family (e.g., sending birthday money or splitting a dinner bill).

Tip: Set up reminders or alerts so you don't forget bill due dates.

Transferring Money Safely

- **Zelle** (built into many banking apps) lets you send money to people you trust using just their phone number or email.

- **Venmo** and **Cash App** are also popular but have social features, so check privacy settings.

- **Never send money to someone you don't know** or to an unfamiliar online seller.

5.3 Budgeting and Expense Tracker Apps

Knowing where your money goes each month helps you stay in control and avoid surprises. Fortunately, there are apps designed to help you **track expenses**, **set budgets**, and **save money**.

Popular Budgeting Apps for Seniors

1. **Mint** (mint.intuit.com)

   o Free and easy to use.

   o Connects to your bank accounts and credit cards.

   o Automatically categorizes your spending (groceries, gas, utilities, etc.).

   o Sends alerts when bills are due or if you overspend.

2. **YNAB (You Need A Budget)** – For more hands-on users.

   o Helps you plan every dollar.

   o Offers tutorials and classes.

   o Paid subscription but offers a free trial.

3. **GoodBudget**

   o Based on the "envelope method."

   o You set aside money for categories like food, gas, entertainment, etc.

   o Easy visual interface.

4. **PocketGuard**

   o Shows how much money you have "left to spend" after bills and savings.

   o Helps spot recurring subscriptions you might have forgotten.

Tip: Choose one app and use it for a few weeks. The more consistent you are, the more helpful the insights will be.

5.4 Shopping Online with Confidence

Online shopping opens a world of convenience—whether you're ordering groceries, clothes, gifts, or medications. However, it's important to **shop safely** and recognize signs of fraud.

Where to Shop Online

1. **Trusted Retailers:**

   o   Amazon, Walmart, Target, Best Buy, and local grocery stores.

   o   Always type the website directly or use their official app.

2. **Specialty Shops:**

   o   Etsy (handmade items)

   o   Chewy (pet supplies)

   o   CVS or Walgreens (pharmacy needs)

3. **Grocery Delivery:**

   o   Instacart, Shipt, or your supermarket's app.

Making Secure Purchases

- Use a **credit card or secure payment service** (PayPal) for added protection.

- Avoid websites that ask for **money transfers** or **gift cards** as payment—these are red flags.

- Look for "https://" in the website address and a small **padlock symbol**—this means the site is secure.

- Save your **order confirmation** and keep a record of purchases.

Red Flags to Watch Out For

- Prices that are "too good to be true."

- Spelling errors or blurry logos on the website.

- No customer service contact information.

- Sellers who pressure you to buy quickly.

Tip: If unsure about a website, check reviews or ask a trusted friend or family member for help.

Managing Deliveries

- You can track packages through shipping confirmation emails.

- Amazon and other retailers allow you to choose delivery times or pick-up options.

- Many services offer **free returns**, making it easy to send things back if they don't fit or aren't what you expected.

In Summary

Learning how to handle your finances online may seem intimidating at first, but it offers huge advantages: **fewer trips to the bank, easier bill payments, better budget control,** and the **freedom to shop from home**.

Here's a recap of what we covered:

- Set up online banking with strong security in place.

- Pay bills and transfer money conveniently, but safely.

- Use budgeting apps like Mint or GoodBudget to track where your money goes.

- Shop online with care—only on secure, well-known sites.

With just a little practice, you'll become more confident and empowered to take full control of your digital finances.

Up Next: In Chapter 6, we'll explore **Digital Health & Wellness**—how to use apps to track medications, book doctor appointments, and stay on top of your health.

Chapter 6: Health and Wellness Apps

In this digital age, technology doesn't just entertain or connect us—it can also help us live healthier, longer, and more fulfilling lives. With the right apps and devices, you can track your steps, manage medications, consult with doctors without leaving your home, and even support your mental well-being.

This chapter explores how seniors can benefit from using health and wellness apps safely and effectively. Whether you're just starting your digital journey or looking to do more with your devices, these tools can help you take control of your health—right from your phone or tablet.

6.1 Using Fitness Trackers and Step Counters

Staying active is vital to healthy aging, and fitness trackers make it easier to set goals and stick with them. You don't have to be a gym-goer or a marathon runner—just walking regularly can make a big difference.

What Are Fitness Trackers?

Fitness trackers, like **Fitbit**, **Apple Watch**, or **Garmin**, are wearable devices that track:

- Steps taken

- Distance walked

- Calories burned

- Heart rate

- Sleep quality

Even if you don't wear a tracker, your **smartphone** likely has a built-in step counter. For example:

- **iPhone:** Health app

- **Android:** Google Fit

Popular Fitness Apps for Seniors

- **Fitbit App** – Syncs with your tracker and provides an overview of your daily activity.

- **Google Fit** – For Android users, tracks movement and integrates with other wellness apps.

- **Pacer** – Easy-to-use pedometer and walking app that doesn't require a separate device.

Tip: Set simple goals, like 5,000 steps a day, and increase slowly. Apps let you see progress and celebrate small wins.

6.2 Medication Reminder and Management Apps

Managing multiple medications can be overwhelming—especially when you need to take different pills at different times. Fortunately, there are apps designed to help you **remember, organize, and even refill prescriptions** easily.

Medication Management Apps

1. **Medisafe**

    o Reminds you when to take each medication.

- o Alerts you if you miss a dose.

- o Tracks your adherence and can notify a family member if desired.

2. **MyTherapy**

   - o Combines medication reminders with health tracking (blood pressure, weight).

   - o Offers printable reports for your doctor.

3. **Pill Reminder – Meds Alarm**

   - o Simple interface, ideal for non-tech-savvy users.

   - o Lets you input multiple meds and schedule alarms.

4. **CareZone** (Note: Discontinued in some areas, but previously useful)

   - o Allowed you to scan your pill bottles and schedule reminders.

Pro Tip: Involve a family member or caregiver when setting up the app to ensure accuracy and peace of mind.

6.3 Telehealth and Virtual Doctor Visits

One of the biggest game-changers in healthcare is **telehealth**—the ability to talk to your doctor via video or phone, without leaving your home. It's especially helpful for seniors with mobility challenges or during times when in-person visits are risky (such as during flu season or a pandemic).

What You Need

- A smartphone, tablet, or laptop with a camera

- A strong Wi-Fi connection

- A secure telehealth app or a link from your doctor's office

Common Telehealth Platforms

1. **MyChart**

   o Connects you to your healthcare provider's network.

   o Lets you schedule appointments, see test results, and have virtual visits.

2. **Teladoc Health**

   o 24/7 access to licensed doctors.

   o Useful for urgent care issues like colds, rashes, and minor infections.

3. **Amwell / MDLIVE**

   o On-demand doctor consultations.

   o Offers therapy and psychiatry services as well.

4. **Doctor on Demand**

   o Highly rated for ease of use.

   o Offers general medicine and mental health appointments.

Telehealth Tips

- Prepare questions in advance, just like you would for an in-person visit.

- Keep your medication list handy.

- Sit in a quiet, well-lit room.

- Test your device and internet beforehand.

Note: Many insurance plans, including Medicare, now cover telehealth visits.

6.4 Mental Wellness and Meditation Apps

Mental health is just as important as physical health. Whether you want to reduce stress, improve your sleep, or simply find a few quiet minutes each day, **mental wellness apps** can help you stay centered.

Benefits of Meditation and Mindfulness

- Lowers stress and anxiety

- Improves focus and memory

- Encourages better sleep

- Promotes emotional well-being

Popular Mental Wellness Apps

1. **Calm**

   o Offers guided meditations, relaxing music, and "sleep stories."

   o Great for beginners and includes sessions just a few minutes long.

2. **Headspace**

   o Simple guided exercises for mindfulness and breathing.

   o Covers topics like stress, anxiety, and focus.

3. **Insight Timer**

   o Free library of over 100,000 meditations.

   o Offers music, talks, and group meditations.

4. **Breathe2Relax**

- o Focuses on breathing techniques to reduce stress.

- o Developed by the U.S. Department of Defense—simple and effective.

5. **Moodfit**

- o Tracks mood, sleep, and habits.

- o Includes gratitude journals and breathing tools.

Getting Started: Try a 5-minute meditation in the morning or evening. The key is consistency, not perfection.

Bonus: Integrating Health Apps with Devices

Many health apps can work together. For example, your Fitbit data may sync with your Apple Health app, or your doctor may access your medication tracker during a telehealth visit. Here's how to make the most of it:

- **Connect your apps to a central hub.** Apple users can use the Health app; Android users can use Google Fit.

- **Share your data with healthcare providers** when relevant—many apps generate printable or digital reports.

- **Set up daily health routines** using reminders and checklists within the app.

In Summary

Technology can be a powerful ally in helping you live a healthier, more active life. From counting your steps to seeing your doctor virtually, these tools are designed to make health management **easier, more accessible, and more consistent** for seniors.

Here's a quick recap:

- Use **fitness trackers** or step-counter apps to stay active.

- Set up **medication reminders** to manage your prescriptions.

- Take advantage of **telehealth apps** for convenient doctor visits from home.

- Explore **mental wellness apps** to reduce stress and improve sleep.

Remember: Start with one small change—whether that's walking a bit more, taking your meds on time, or breathing deeply for five minutes. Over time, these habits can make a big impact on your well-being.

Coming Up in Chapter 7: We'll explore **Learning and Hobbies Online**—how to use technology to explore new interests, take classes, and find communities who share your passions.

Chapter 7: Organizing Daily Life with Apps

As life gets busier, even in retirement, staying organized can be a challenge. Between doctor appointments, family gatherings, grocery shopping, and daily chores, it's easy to forget small (but important) tasks. Luckily, there's a digital solution for that! With just a smartphone or tablet, you can use apps to **keep track of your schedule, manage grocery lists, jot down important notes, and even plan your meals.**

Let's explore how these everyday tools can make your life easier, more structured, and a lot less stressful.

7.1 Calendar and Reminder Tools

Why Use a Digital Calendar?

A digital calendar helps you remember appointments, birthdays, family events, and more. No more flipping through paper planners or sticky notes. Once you add an event to your calendar, you can set reminders, invite others, and even receive notifications before it starts.

Popular Calendar Apps

1. **Google Calendar (Free)**

    o Syncs across devices (phone, tablet, computer).

    o Add appointments with dates, times, and alerts.

    o Color-code events (e.g., blue for medical, green for social).

    o Share events with family.

2. **Apple Calendar (Free for iPhone/iPad users)**

   o Built into your device.

   o Integrates with Siri: "Hey Siri, remind me of my dentist appointment next Monday at 10 a.m."

   o Simple interface with daily, weekly, and monthly views.

3. **Microsoft Outlook Calendar**

   o Especially useful if you already use Outlook for email.

   o Easy to organize events and send invites.

Reminder Apps

- **Google Keep or Apple Reminders** – Add a quick task like "take medicine at 8 PM."

- **Alarm Clock Apps** – Use them for regular reminders like drinking water or standing up every hour.

- **Pill Reminder by Medisafe** – Combines medication management with reminders.

Tip: Set recurring events for weekly routines, like church service or a phone call with grandkids.

7.2 Grocery and To-Do List Apps

Ever gone to the store and forgotten what you needed? Or remembered a task after it was too late? Digital **to-do lists** and **grocery list apps** can help you keep everything in one place—no paper needed!

To-Do List Apps

1. **Todoist**

   o   Simple and beautifully designed.

   o   Organize tasks into categories like "Home," "Errands," "Doctor."

   o   Check off completed items (so satisfying!).

2. **Microsoft To Do**

   o   Syncs with Windows computers.

   o   Set reminders, due dates, and repeat tasks.

3. **Google Keep**

   o   Combines checklists with notes and photos.

   o   Use voice commands to add new items.

4. **Any.do**

   o   Combines a to-do list, calendar, and reminder tool in one.

   o   Has voice input and syncing across devices.

Grocery List Apps

1. **Our Groceries**

   o   Share your list with a spouse or caregiver.

   o   As items are added or checked off, it updates in real time.

2. **Bring!**

   o   Easy-to-use interface with large icons.

   o   Group items by type (dairy, produce, snacks).

3. **Out of Milk**

   o   Makes grocery and pantry lists.

   o   Includes barcode scanning.

Pro Tip: Keep a running grocery list on your phone. As soon as you run out of something, add it with a few taps.

7.3 Notes and Voice Memo Tools

Sometimes, you just want to jot something down: a phone number, a book recommendation, or an idea that pops into your head. Instead of searching for a pen and paper, use your phone or tablet.

Note-Taking Apps

1. **Evernote**

   o   Save text, photos, and voice notes.

   o   Organize notes into folders for topics like "Health," "Family," or "Travel."

2. **Apple Notes**

   o   Built into iPhones and iPads.

   o   Syncs with iCloud, so you can access notes on all devices.

3. **Google Keep**

   o   Sticky-note style with colors and labels.

   o   Add checklists, reminders, or even drawings.

4. **Simplenote**

- o Clean, no-frills interface.

- o Great for quick thoughts and syncing across platforms.

Voice Memo Tools

1. **Apple Voice Memos**

   - o Record your thoughts by speaking instead of typing.

   - o Save recordings to play back later.

2. **Easy Voice Recorder (Android)**

   - o Tap to start/stop recording.

   - o Rename and organize audio clips.

3. **Google Assistant or Siri**

   - o Just say, "Hey Google, take a note," or "Siri, remind me to call the doctor."

Tip: Use voice memos if you have arthritis or find typing difficult. It's quick, easy, and hands-free.

7.4 Meal Planning and Recipe Apps

Cooking can be joyful, but deciding what to cook can be a daily struggle. Meal planning apps make it easier to organize meals, find recipes, and even create a grocery list based on the ingredients needed.

Meal Planning Apps

1. **Mealime**

   - o Choose from healthy, senior-friendly recipes.

- o Adjust for dietary needs (low salt, low sugar, vegetarian).

- o Automatically generates a grocery list.

2. **Paprika**

- o Save recipes from websites.

- o Create weekly meal plans.

- o Track ingredients you already have in your pantry.

3. **Plan to Eat**

- o Organize recipes and plan meals on a calendar.

- o Share meal plans with family.

4. **Yummly**

- o Search by ingredient or dietary restriction.

- o Step-by-step cooking instructions.

- o Voice control to go hands-free while cooking.

Recipe Discovery Apps

1. **Tasty**

- o Fun, video-based recipes.

- o Good for visual learners who like to follow along.

2. **AllRecipes**

- o Large community of home cooks.

- o Filter recipes by cooking time, ingredients, and reviews.

3. **BigOven**

   o Find new meals based on what's already in your fridge.

   o Add meals to a built-in planner.

Cooking for one? Look for apps with small-serving options or leftovers-friendly recipes.

Final Thoughts: Digital Tools for a Smoother Daily Routine

Incorporating technology into your daily life doesn't have to be overwhelming—it can actually make things **simpler and more manageable**. Whether you're keeping track of medical appointments, grocery lists, or your favorite recipes, there's an app that can support you every step of the way.

Let's recap how to stay organized with your devices:

- Use **calendars** to manage appointments and recurring events.

- Keep **to-do and grocery lists** to stay on top of daily tasks.

- Use **notes and voice memos** to capture ideas and reminders on the go.

- Plan meals and discover new dishes with **recipe and meal planning apps**.

The best part? These tools are customizable to your needs and grow with you over time. Even a small habit—like checking your calendar each morning or planning meals on Sunday—can lead to big improvements in your daily routine.

Next Up in Chapter 8: We'll cover **Entertainment and Leisure Online**—how to stream movies, listen to music, play games, and explore hobbies all from the comfort of your home.

Chapter 8: Exploring Entertainment and Hobbies

Technology isn't just about staying connected or managing your calendar—it's also about **having fun**. Whether you're watching a favorite movie, discovering new music, playing mind-sharpening games, or joining a community of people who share your hobbies, the digital world offers endless opportunities for entertainment and enrichment.

In this chapter, we'll guide you through how to enjoy your favorite pastimes online, discover new ones, and make every day a little more joyful—all with a tap or a click.

8.1 Watching Movies and Shows (Netflix, Prime Video, YouTube)

Gone are the days when you had to wait for your favorite show to air at a specific time. Streaming platforms allow you to watch movies and TV shows anytime, anywhere. Whether you're into classic films, documentaries, or new releases, there's something for everyone.

Popular Streaming Services

1. **Netflix**

   o Offers thousands of movies and shows across genres.

   o Includes documentaries, foreign films, and Netflix Originals.

   o Easy to use, with personalized suggestions.

   o Monthly subscription required.

2. **Amazon Prime Video**

- Comes with an Amazon Prime membership.

- Includes a wide variety of movies, TV shows, and original content.

- Offers some free and some rental-only titles.

3. **YouTube**

- Great for free videos: music, how-tos, documentaries, and classic films.

- Search for shows, old concerts, cooking tutorials, and more.

- No subscription required, but ad-free experience available via YouTube Premium.

4. **Other Options**:

- **Disney+** for family and animated content.

- **Hulu** for current shows and next-day TV.

- **Tubi and Pluto TV** for free, ad-supported streaming.

Tip: Use closed captions or subtitles for easier understanding, especially if you're hard of hearing.

8.2 Listening to Music and Podcasts

Music has a powerful way of lifting spirits and bringing back memories. And podcasts? They're like radio shows on demand—on topics ranging from history and storytelling to wellness and humor.

Music Apps

1. **Spotify**

- Listen to your favorite songs, create playlists, and explore new genres.

- o Offers both free (with ads) and premium versions.

2. **Apple Music**

   - o Perfect for iPhone and iPad users.

   - o Extensive library and curated playlists.

   - o Subscription required.

3. **Amazon Music**

   - o Free with a Prime subscription.

   - o Easy to search by artist, genre, or mood.

4. **YouTube Music**

   - o Great for watching music videos or listening on the go.

Podcasts: Talk Radio for the Digital Age

1. **Spotify Podcasts**

   - o Browse thousands of free shows: true crime, health, travel, comedy, and more.

2. **Apple Podcasts**

   - o Pre-installed on iPhones and iPads.

   - o Organized by category for easy browsing.

3. **Google Podcasts**

   - o Simple and user-friendly.

   - o Works well on Android devices.

Tip: Try a podcast like "The Daily," "Stuff You Should Know," or "Good Life Project" to start your journey.

8.3 Playing Games for Brain Health

Games aren't just for kids—they're a fantastic way to **stay mentally sharp**, reduce stress, and have fun. From word puzzles and memory games to online card games with friends, digital gaming is a great hobby for seniors.

Brain-Training and Puzzle Games

1. **Lumosity**

   o Designed by neuroscientists to train memory, attention, and problem-solving.

   o Daily exercises customized to your performance.

2. **Elevate**

   o Focuses on communication and analytical skills.

   o Tracks your progress and improves over time.

3. **Peak**

   o Offers short, engaging games to boost mental agility.

   o Great for quick play sessions.

Fun and Casual Games

1. **Words With Friends**

   o Online version of Scrabble you can play with friends or strangers.

   o Helps with vocabulary and spelling.

2. **Solitaire, Sudoku, and Mahjong**

   o   Available as apps or online.

   o   Relaxing and mentally engaging.

3. **Jigsaw Puzzle Apps**

   o   Choose the number of pieces and difficulty level.

   o   No need to clean up afterward!

Tip: Set a daily "play break" to keep your brain active and give yourself a fun moment to look forward to.

8.4 Joining Online Groups and Hobby Forums

One of the best parts of the internet is how it connects people who share interests—no matter the distance. Whether you love knitting, gardening, birdwatching, or photography, there's an online group for you.

Social Platforms for Hobby Groups

1. **Facebook Groups**

   o   Join communities for seniors, hobbyists, or specific interests.

   o   Examples: "Knitting for Beginners," "Senior Gardening Club," "Classic Movie Lovers."

2. **Reddit**

   o   A massive forum platform with topic-specific "subreddits."

   o   Example communities: r/Over50, r/Birding, r/Slowcooking, r/Music.

3. **Meetup**

o Find local or virtual hobby groups and events.

o Join book clubs, tech workshops, walking groups, or senior socials.

4. **Nextdoor**

o Connects you with your neighborhood.

o Great for local recommendations, community news, and local events.

Hobby-Specific Apps

- **Pinterest** – Visual inspiration for crafts, gardening, decor, recipes, and more.

- **Ravelry** – A knitting and crochet community with patterns and forums.

- **AllTrails** – For walkers and nature lovers—maps and reviews of local trails.

- **Audubon Bird Guide** – For bird enthusiasts to identify and track sightings.

Tip: Don't be shy—join a group, introduce yourself, and ask questions. Online communities are often friendly and welcoming, especially to newcomers.

Final Thoughts: Entertainment Isn't Just a Pastime—It's a Path to Joy

Technology isn't just for practicality—it's for pleasure too. Embracing digital entertainment can help reduce loneliness, fight boredom, and inspire creativity. Whether you're watching a movie, learning through a podcast, solving puzzles, or sharing your hobby with an online group, you're actively investing in your mental and emotional well-being.

Let's recap some key ideas:

- Use **streaming apps** to enjoy your favorite movies and shows at your pace.

- Discover **new music and podcasts** to stimulate your mind and mood.

- Play **games** to stay sharp and have fun.

- Find your people in **online hobby groups** that connect you with others.

So go ahead—download that puzzle game, join that Facebook birdwatching group, or start a new cooking series on YouTube. Your digital lifestyle isn't just about staying connected—it's about **staying engaged, joyful, and alive**.

Next Up in Chapter 9: We'll talk about **Travel and Transportation Apps**—how to plan trips, book rides, and explore the world using your phone or tablet.

Chapter 9: Learning New Skills Online

One of the most empowering aspects of the digital age is the ability to **learn anything, anytime, anywhere**. Whether it's brushing up on an old passion or diving into a completely new skill, the internet offers endless educational opportunities—many of them free and tailored for people of all ages, including seniors.

Learning isn't just for students—it's for life. Staying mentally engaged promotes brain health, boosts confidence, and brings personal satisfaction. In this chapter, we'll explore some of the best ways to learn new skills online and how to access educational resources from the comfort of your home.

9.1 Using YouTube for Tutorials

YouTube isn't just for funny videos or music—it's one of the most powerful learning tools on the internet. With millions of free tutorials, you can learn nearly any skill you're interested in, from knitting and painting to learning how to use your smartphone more efficiently.

What You Can Learn on YouTube:

- **Tech skills**: Learn how to use apps, set up devices, or fix computer issues.

- **Creative arts**: Drawing, photography, calligraphy, music, or crafting.

- **Cooking tutorials**: Recipes from around the world, cooking for one, or dietary-specific meals.

- **Exercise and yoga**: Tailored workouts for seniors, stretching, or low-impact fitness.

- **Languages**: Short lessons in Spanish, French, Italian, or any other language.

- **Home improvement**: Simple repairs, gardening tips, or DIY projects.

Tips for Using YouTube Effectively:

- Use the **search bar** to look up exactly what you want. For example, type "How to use Zoom for beginners" or "Easy knitting for seniors."

- Subscribe to channels you enjoy, so you never miss a new video.

- Use **closed captions (CC)** if you want to follow along more easily.

- Watch at your own pace—pause, rewind, and replay any part.

Some beginner-friendly YouTube channels include:

- **Senior Planet** – Tech tips for older adults.

- **Yoga with Adriene** – Gentle yoga for all ages.

- **Cooking with Brenda Gantt** – Traditional home-style cooking.

- **The Great Courses Plus** – Lectures and lifelong learning.

9.2 Free Learning Platforms (Coursera, Khan Academy, Duolingo)

If you're looking for a more structured way to learn, many websites offer full courses in a wide variety of subjects. The best part? Many of them are **completely free** or offer free options.

Coursera

- Offers free and paid courses from top universities like Yale, Stanford, and more.

- Topics include history, art, technology, business, and health.

- You can audit courses for free or pay for a certificate.

- Easy-to-follow video lectures with optional subtitles.

Khan Academy

- 100% free and highly respected.

- Focuses on math, science, economics, and life skills.

- Offers step-by-step lessons for all levels.

- Includes interactive quizzes to test your knowledge.

Duolingo

- A fun and free way to learn a new language.

- Offers lessons in Spanish, French, German, Italian, and more.

- Uses a game-like format that makes learning feel like play.

- Tracks your progress and sends reminders to practice.

Other Honorable Mentions:

- **edX** – Courses from MIT, Harvard, and more.

- **Skillshare** – Creative and practical skills, like photography, graphic design, or writing (free trial available).

- **FutureLearn** – British-based learning platform with global content.

Tip: Choose one course or app to focus on at a time. Don't overwhelm yourself—learning should be enjoyable, not stressful!

9.3 Virtual Libraries and eBooks

If you love reading or want to dive into a new subject, your local library may offer free access to thousands of **eBooks, audiobooks, and learning resources**—all online.

How to Access Virtual Libraries

- **OverDrive (Libby App)**

    o Borrow books and audiobooks just like at a physical library.

    o Works on smartphones, tablets, and computers.

    o All you need is a library card.

- **Hoopla**

    o Another free library service offering books, movies, music, and more.

    o Often included with your public library membership.

- **Project Gutenberg**

    o Access over 60,000 free public domain books.

    o Great for reading classics like Charles Dickens, Jane Austen, or Mark Twain.

- **Google Books & Amazon Kindle**

    o Browse free and paid eBooks.

    o Many Kindle books are free or cost just a few dollars.

o You don't need a Kindle device—you can read on your phone or tablet.

Tip: Prefer to listen instead of read? Try audiobooks—perfect for resting your eyes while staying informed or entertained.

9.4 Lifelong Learning Communities for Seniors

Learning is always more enjoyable when shared with others. Luckily, the internet makes it easy to join communities of other seniors who are also eager to learn. Whether it's through live virtual classes, discussion groups, or hobby workshops, being part of a learning community can motivate you and help you form new friendships.

Senior-Focused Learning Communities

1. **Senior Planet**

   o Offers free online classes for older adults on everything from technology to wellness.

   o Hosts live Zoom workshops where you can ask questions and interact.

   o Topics include "Intro to YouTube," "Online Safety," and "Digital Art."

2. **Oasis Everywhere**

   o Online learning tailored for adults over 50.

   o Classes on history, science, current events, arts, and health.

   o Small class sizes and interactive discussions.

3. **GetSetUp**

   o Live and interactive classes for seniors, taught by seniors.

- o Focus on technology, hobbies, and life skills.

- o Some free classes and some paid.

4. **Lifelong Learning Institutes (LLIs)**

   - o Many universities and community colleges offer LLI programs.

   - o Includes both online and in-person learning.

   - o You can take non-credit courses with no pressure—just pure learning!

Tip: Look for programs through your local university or library. Many offer free or low-cost classes specifically for retirees.

Final Thoughts: It's Never Too Late to Learn

In this digital age, curiosity has no age limit. Whether you're discovering a new hobby, diving into history, learning a language, or mastering a tech skill, there's a world of knowledge waiting for you online.

Let's recap the key takeaways from this chapter:

- **YouTube** is a goldmine for free, beginner-friendly tutorials on nearly any topic.

- **Learning platforms** like Coursera, Khan Academy, and Duolingo make structured education accessible and enjoyable.

- **Virtual libraries** and eBooks keep your mind active without leaving home.

- **Senior learning communities** help you learn alongside others while making new connections.

Lifelong learning is about more than acquiring facts—it's about exploring the world with curiosity, confidence, and joy. So whether you're 60 or 90, now is the perfect time to pick up a new skill or passion. The tools are in your hands—and your next adventure is only a click away.

Coming Up in Chapter 10: We'll explore how seniors can safely and easily **navigate travel and transportation apps**, from booking a ride with Uber to checking public transit schedules and planning trips online.

Chapter 10: Digital Safety and Security

As we spend more time online—whether for connecting with family, learning new skills, or managing our finances—it's essential to understand how to **stay safe and protect personal information**. Digital safety and security might sound technical, but it's easier than you think when you know the basics.

In this chapter, we'll cover key topics like creating strong passwords, avoiding online scams, managing your privacy settings, and backing up important information. These steps will help you navigate the internet with more confidence and peace of mind.

10.1 Creating Strong Passwords

Your password is the first line of defense in protecting your personal data. A weak password is like leaving your front door unlocked. Unfortunately, many people use easy-to-guess passwords like "123456" or "password." These are the first ones hackers try.

What Makes a Strong Password?

- **At least 12 characters long**
- A mix of **uppercase and lowercase letters**
- Includes **numbers and special characters** (like !, @, $, %)
- Avoid using your **name, birthday, or pet's name**

Example of a strong password: SunSh1ne$2025!Lemon

Password Tips:

- Don't reuse the same password for multiple accounts. If one account is hacked, the rest could be vulnerable.

- Use a **password manager** like LastPass, 1Password, or Bitwarden to remember complex passwords for you.

- Change your passwords regularly, especially for sensitive accounts like email and banking.

Tip: Write down your passwords in a safe place if you're not comfortable using a digital manager. Just don't leave them near your computer.

10.2 Avoiding Online Scams and Phishing

Online scams are becoming more sophisticated, targeting people of all ages. But with awareness, you can avoid the traps set by cybercriminals. One of the most common tactics is **phishing**—fake emails or messages that try to trick you into giving away personal information.

What is Phishing?

Phishing is when someone pretends to be a trusted source—like your bank, email provider, or even a friend—to get you to:

- Click on a harmful link

- Download a malicious attachment

- Enter your login or financial information

Warning Signs of Scams and Phishing:

- **Urgency**: "Your account will be closed unless you act now!"

- **Spelling and grammar mistakes**

- **Suspicious email addresses** like support@abc-bank123.com

- **Links that look off**: Always hover over a link (without clicking) to see the full address

How to Protect Yourself:

- Never click on suspicious links or download unknown attachments.

- Don't share your Social Security Number, credit card info, or passwords over email or text.

- When in doubt, **contact the company directly** using a trusted phone number or website—not the one in the email or text.

Tip: If you receive a suspicious message from a friend or family member, call them to confirm. Their account might have been hacked.

10.3 Managing Privacy Settings on Apps and Websites

Every time you sign up for a new app or website, you share bits of personal information. It's important to **control who can see this data** and how it's used. Thankfully, most apps let you adjust your **privacy settings**—you just need to know where to look.

What Are Privacy Settings?

Privacy settings let you control:

- What personal information is visible to others (like your birthdate, location, or phone number)

- Who can contact you or see your posts

- What kind of data the app collects about your activity

How to Check and Adjust Privacy Settings:

On Facebook:

- Go to "Settings & Privacy" → "Privacy Checkup"

- Limit who can see your posts to "Friends" only

- Review what apps are connected to your Facebook account

On Google:

- Visit myaccount.google.com

- Review "Privacy & Personalization"

- Manage location tracking, ad settings, and search history

On Smartphones (iPhone/Android):

- Open "Settings" → "Privacy"

- See which apps have access to your location, camera, microphone, or contacts

- Turn off permissions for apps you don't trust or use

Tip: Be cautious about "Sign in with Facebook" or "Sign in with Google" on other websites. This can share your info across platforms.

10.4 Backing Up Important Information

Just like you keep paper copies of important documents, it's vital to back up your **digital information**. Backups ensure that if your device is lost, stolen, or stops working, your photos, contacts, and files are still safe.

What is a Backup?

A backup is a **copy** of your files or data that's stored in another place, such as:

- **The cloud** (online storage)

- **An external hard drive** or USB stick

- **Another device**, like a second computer or phone

What to Back Up:

- Photos and videos

- Contacts and address books

- Important documents (PDFs, Word files, etc.)

- Emails, if needed for legal or personal reasons

How to Back Up Your Data:

1. Use Cloud Storage Services

- **Google Drive** (15GB free with Gmail)

- **iCloud** (built into iPhones and iPads)

- **Dropbox**, **OneDrive**, or **Amazon Photos**

2. Use an External Storage Device

- Purchase a small external hard drive or USB flash drive.

- Plug it into your computer and drag files to copy them over.

3. Enable Automatic Backups

- On iPhone: Settings → [Your Name] → iCloud → iCloud Backup → Turn On

- On Android: Settings → Google → Backup → Turn On

Tip: Back up your data at least once a month or set it to happen automatically.

Final Thoughts: Stay Smart, Stay Safe

Being online offers incredible benefits, but just like the real world, it requires a bit of caution. Digital safety isn't about being afraid—it's about being informed and prepared. Whether you're browsing the web, shopping, chatting, or managing finances, these safety habits help keep your identity, money, and peace of mind protected.

Let's review the key lessons from this chapter:

- **Strong passwords** protect your accounts—use a mix of characters and avoid personal details.

- **Scams and phishing** are common—stay skeptical of messages asking for urgent action or sensitive info.

- **Privacy settings** give you control over what others can see—adjust them regularly.

- **Backups** ensure your memories and important files aren't lost—use the cloud or a backup device.

Taking a few minutes to strengthen your digital habits can make a huge difference. You don't need to be a tech expert—just a little awareness and routine can keep you safe and secure online.

 Up Next in Chapter 11: We'll explore how to use **transportation and travel apps**, helping you book rides, plan trips, and explore the world right from your fingertips.

Chapter 11: Staying Connected with Family

One of the most heartwarming and meaningful uses of technology is its ability to help us **stay connected with loved ones**, no matter the distance. Whether you're a grandparent living miles away from your grandchildren, a parent coordinating family activities, or just someone who wants to feel close to family members, today's digital tools offer many simple and fun ways to keep those relationships strong.

In this chapter, we'll explore how to share photos and memories, use family apps for coordination and safety, enjoy tech-based activities with younger generations, and even host virtual family gatherings that bring everyone together.

11.1 Sharing Photo Albums and Memories

There's nothing like a good photo to spark conversation and warm the heart. Sharing pictures, especially with family members who live far away, is one of the easiest and most joyful ways to stay in touch.

How to Share Photos Easily:

1. Google Photos

- Upload pictures from your phone or computer.

- Create shared albums where family members can view and add their own photos.

- Use facial recognition to sort photos by person automatically.

2. Apple Photos

- For iPhone or iPad users, iCloud Photo Sharing lets you create albums and invite family members to view or contribute.

- You can add captions and "like" photos, just like on social media.

3. Facebook or Instagram (Private Sharing)

- Create a private group or page just for family.

- Share photos, videos, or even live moments with select people.

- Comment and react to stay engaged with what everyone's up to.

Tips for Meaningful Sharing:

- Organize albums by events (e.g., "Grandma's Birthday," "Summer Vacation").

- Add brief descriptions or stories to the photos.

- Encourage younger family members to share their own updates—it becomes a two-way street.

Idea: Start a "Throwback Thursday" family album where everyone shares old family photos and memories each week.

11.2 Using Family Apps (Life360, Shared Calendars)

Families are busy, and it can be tricky to keep up with everyone's schedule or whereabouts. Fortunately, family-focused apps are designed to help everyone stay in sync and feel connected.

Life360 – Location Sharing and Safety

Life360 is a popular family locator app:

- Shows real-time locations of family members.

- Alerts you when someone arrives or leaves a place (like school, home, or work).

- Includes driving reports, emergency SOS, and even crash detection.

Helpful for peace of mind, especially for older adults or teens on the go.

Shared Calendars – Stay on Schedule

Apps like **Google Calendar** or **Cozi Family Organizer** let everyone share events:

- Add doctor appointments, school events, birthdays, and family outings.

- Sync across multiple devices.

- Set reminders and color-code events by family member.

Cozi also includes grocery lists, to-dos, and meal planning—all in one place.

Group Messaging Apps

- Use **WhatsApp**, **GroupMe**, or **Messenger** to create family group chats.

- Share updates, links, and pictures in real-time.

- Pin important messages like Wi-Fi passwords or emergency contacts.

11.3 Grandparent-Grandchild Tech Activities

Technology can bridge the generation gap in delightful ways. Grandparents and grandchildren can bond through games, creative projects, and learning tools—even if they aren't in the same room.

Playing Games Together

Many online games are safe, fun, and offer great opportunities for connection:

- **Words with Friends** – A Scrabble-like word game you can play turn by turn.

- **Uno**, **Checkers**, or **Chess apps** – Classic games with a tech twist.

- **Animal Crossing** or **Minecraft** – Let younger grandkids show you around in their digital worlds.

Creating Together

- **Art apps** like Tayasui Sketches or Doodle Buddy let you draw and color together.

- Use video calls while doing crafts, puzzles, or reading stories aloud.

- Share creative projects through photos or even start a shared scrapbook.

Learning Side-by-Side

- Watch educational YouTube channels together.

- Try Duolingo and learn a new language as a team.

- Explore online museums or virtual tours together.

Idea: Start a "virtual book club" with your grandchildren. Read the same story and discuss it over Zoom or FaceTime.

11.4 Hosting Virtual Family Events

Technology allows families to **celebrate milestones and stay socially active** even when distance or health concerns keep them apart. From casual get-togethers to holiday dinners, virtual events are here to stay—and they're surprisingly easy to organize.

Tools to Use:

- **Zoom**: Easy-to-use video conferencing with options for screen sharing and breakout rooms.

- **Google Meet** or **FaceTime**: Great for smaller gatherings.

- **Facebook Rooms**: Casual video chats with built-in games and filters.

Event Ideas:

- **Virtual Family Reunions**: Set a date, send out invites, and let everyone share updates and stories.

- **Birthday Celebrations**: Coordinate cake and decorations, sing Happy Birthday, and watch the birthday person open gifts on camera.

- **Game Nights**: Play charades, trivia, or online games together.

- **Holiday Gatherings**: Cook the same meal in different kitchens and eat together over video.

How to Make It Feel Special:

- Send a "party package" ahead of time (hats, balloons, snacks).

- Create a playlist and play music during the call.

- Design a digital invitation using tools like Canva or Evite.

Tip: Designate a "tech helper" in the family who can assist older or less tech-savvy members with setup and troubleshooting before events.

Final Thoughts: Love, Laughter, and Lifelong Bonds

Technology doesn't replace the warmth of an in-person hug or the joy of shared laughter around a table—but it does help bridge the gap between those moments. By using the tools covered in this chapter, you can stay close to family, create new traditions, and build meaningful memories across the miles.

Whether it's a simple photo, a shared calendar, a bedtime story over video call, or a grand virtual family party, these moments make us feel seen, loved, and connected.

Key Takeaways:

- **Photo sharing** apps help you preserve and enjoy family memories together.

- **Family organization tools** like Life360 and shared calendars keep everyone informed and coordinated.

- **Tech activities with grandchildren** encourage fun, learning, and bonding.

- **Virtual events** can bring the whole family together, no matter the distance.

Staying connected isn't just about the technology—it's about the love behind it.

Next up in Chapter 12: We'll explore **travel and transportation apps** that help you get around town, plan trips, or even book a ride—all from your device.

Chapter 12: Troubleshooting and Finding Help

No matter how simple or advanced your device is, chances are you'll run into a problem or two. A frozen screen, a forgotten password, or a mysterious error message—these things happen. But the good news is, you don't have to be a tech expert to solve most everyday issues. With a little patience and the right tools, you can become your own tech hero.

In this chapter, we'll walk through **common tech problems and simple fixes**, how to use **Google and YouTube to find helpful tutorials**, when and how to reach **trusted tech support**, and where to turn for **friendly, ongoing tech help made especially for seniors**.

12.1 Common Tech Problems and Fixes

Let's start with the basics—those everyday issues that can seem intimidating at first but often have very simple solutions.

Problem 1: Device Won't Turn On

- **Try This**: Make sure the device is charged. Plug it in and wait a few minutes.

- Check for a **power indicator light**. If it doesn't light up, try a different charger or outlet.

- For computers, hold the **power button** down for 10 seconds and try again.

Problem 2: No Internet Connection

- **Try This**: Restart your modem/router by unplugging it for 30 seconds, then plugging it back in.

- Restart your device.

- Check if **Wi-Fi is turned on** in your settings and connected to the correct network.

Problem 3: Forgot a Password

- **Try This**: Look for a "Forgot Password?" link on the login page.

- Follow the prompts to reset it using your email or phone number.

- Use a password manager (like LastPass or Apple's built-in Keychain) to store passwords securely.

Problem 4: Device is Running Slowly

- **Try This**: Close unused apps or browser tabs.

- Restart your device.

- Delete old files or apps you no longer use to free up space.

- Check for software updates—sometimes, performance issues are solved with a quick update.

□ Problem 5: Printer Not Working

- **Try This**: Make sure it's powered on and connected (via Wi-Fi or USB).

- Restart both the printer and your computer.

- Check for any paper jams.

- Reinstall the printer driver if needed.

Tip: Keep a small notebook where you write down common fixes that worked for you—it can be a lifesaver next time!

12.2 Using Google and YouTube to Find Solutions

One of the best tools for solving tech problems is **simply searching for them online**. You don't need fancy language or technical terms—just describe the issue in plain words.

Using Google Search

When you run into a tech issue:

- Open your browser and go to www.google.com.

- Type your problem in the search bar, such as:

    o *"iPad won't connect to Wi-Fi"*

    o *"How to recover Gmail password"*

    o *"Phone screen too dark how to fix"*

Google will often provide direct answers, step-by-step guides, or video tutorials.

YouTube: Your Visual Guide

YouTube is fantastic for visual learners.

- Visit www.youtube.com.

- In the search bar, type your problem or question.

- Look for videos with clear titles, high ratings, and many views.

- Watch a few different videos to see which one is easiest to follow.

Tip: Add your device's name or model when searching (e.g., "Samsung Galaxy S10 won't charge")
to get more accurate help.

12.3 Getting Help from Trusted Tech Support

Sometimes, a problem is too tricky or frustrating to solve on your own—and that's okay! When you need more help, it's important to **reach out to trusted sources** and avoid scams.

Beware of Fake Tech Support

- If a pop-up tells you to call a number because your computer has a "virus," it's **likely a scam**.

- Never give your passwords or remote access to someone you don't know.

- If someone calls claiming to be from Microsoft, Apple, or Amazon asking for your information—**hang up**.

Trusted Tech Support Options:

1. Manufacturer Support:

- **Apple Support**: support.apple.com

- **Samsung Support**: samsung.com/us/support

- **Microsoft Support**: support.microsoft.com

2. Internet or Phone Provider:

- Contact your service provider for help with internet, landlines, or mobile issues.

3. In-Home Services (Paid):

- Geek Squad (Best Buy) or local tech companies offer in-person assistance.

- Ask a trusted family member to recommend someone.

4. Remote Support (Be Cautious):

- If you do allow remote access, only do it through known companies like Apple, Microsoft, or your internet provider.

Tip: Keep a list of support phone numbers or websites in a notebook or printed out and placed near your device.

12.4 Local Tech Classes and Online Communities for Seniors

Learning is easier—and a lot more fun—when done with others. Many communities now offer **technology education specifically for seniors**, both in-person and online. These resources are welcoming, patient, and paced for all experience levels.

Local Resources

1. Libraries

- Many public libraries offer free classes on using smartphones, email, social media, or general computer skills.

- Ask your librarian or check their website for upcoming sessions.

2. Senior Centers

- Local senior centers often provide digital literacy workshops.

- Some offer one-on-one help with volunteers or students.

3. Community Colleges

- Look for adult education or continuing education programs focused on digital skills.

Online Communities and Courses

1. Senior Planet

Website: www.seniorplanet.org

- Offers live virtual classes, tech help, and how-to guides designed for older adults.

- Topics range from Zoom and Facebook to online safety and smart home devices.

2. GetSetUp

Website: www.getsetup.io

- Interactive classes taught by older adults, for older adults.

- Learn everything from using your iPhone to starting a blog.

3. AARP's Technology Guide

Website: www.aarp.org/technology

- Articles, videos, and guides on using digital tools safely and effectively.

Joining Tech Forums

- Forums like **TechBoomers**, **Reddit's r/AskTech**, or even dedicated Facebook groups offer friendly help.

- Ask questions, share experiences, and learn from others—many seniors are there just like you.

Final Thoughts: You've Got This!

Tech troubles can be frustrating—but you are never alone in facing them. With the right mindset, tools, and resources, you can handle common problems with confidence and know where to turn when things get tricky.

Remember: every expert started as a beginner. Every time you fix something or learn a new tool, you're building your confidence and becoming more empowered in the digital world.

Key Takeaways:

- Most everyday tech issues have simple solutions—don't panic!

- Google and YouTube are powerful allies for solving problems.

- Always get support from **trusted** sources and watch for scams.

- Join classes or communities that teach tech skills at your pace and in your style.

Keep this chapter handy as your personal "first aid kit" for tech troubles—and don't be afraid to ask for help. Everyone gets stuck sometimes. The important thing is that you're learning, growing, and staying connected.

Conclusion

Embracing the Digital World at Your Own Pace

Congratulations! By making it to the end of this guide, you've already proven something important: you're more capable and tech-savvy than you may have thought. Whether you're completely new to smartphones, tablets, and apps—or just looking to sharpen your skills—you've taken a big step toward embracing the digital world with curiosity and confidence.

The digital world can feel overwhelming at times. New apps pop up daily, devices get updates, and it can seem like things are always changing. But here's the truth: **you don't have to learn everything all at once**. Technology is not a race—it's a journey, and you're in charge of the pace.

What matters most is that you've taken the first step—and every tap, click, or swipe from here on is a win. Let's reflect on how far you've come and explore what's next.

Encouragement for Continued Exploration

Technology isn't just about gadgets or apps—it's about what they **allow you to do**. From staying in touch with loved ones, to managing your finances, to keeping your health on track, you've learned how the digital world can enhance your life.

If you've ever doubted your ability to keep up, consider all the skills you've gained:

- Sending messages and making video calls.

- Using banking apps and paying bills online.

- Organizing your calendar and shopping lists with ease.

- Finding new hobbies, entertainment, and even lifelong learning opportunities.

- Exploring tools to stay mentally and physically healthy.

And let's not forget—**you've read a whole digital book!** That's already a huge accomplishment.

What you're doing is more than keeping up—you're thriving in a world that is constantly evolving. Remember, even the most experienced tech users encounter problems, forget passwords, or get confused by new updates. The key is to stay **curious, patient, and persistent**.

You're More Tech-Savvy Than You Think!

Many people think being tech-savvy means being an expert or knowing everything about computers and smartphones. But in reality, being tech-savvy just means you're:

- Willing to **learn something new**.

- Unafraid to **ask questions** or seek help.

- Able to **solve everyday problems** using digital tools.

- Comfortable with making mistakes and learning from them.

Even if you don't know how to use every app or feature yet, your mindset is what makes the biggest difference.

Give yourself credit for every step:

- You opened an app today? Great!

- You tried out a budgeting tool or watched a YouTube tutorial? Amazing!

- You Googled something instead of giving up? That's progress!

There's no final destination when it comes to tech—it's about building confidence one click at a time.

Final Tips and Next Steps

Before you go, here are a few friendly tips to help you continue your digital journey with ease:

1. Stick with One New Thing at a Time

Don't try to master everything at once. Pick one app or task to explore this week— maybe it's learning to order groceries online, starting a digital journal, or joining a virtual class. Take your time and enjoy the process.

2. Create a "Tech Buddy" System

Pair up with a friend, neighbor, or grandchild who can help you when you get stuck. Learning together—or having someone just a call away—can make it more fun and less stressful.

3. Use Notes and Reminders

It's perfectly okay to write things down. Keep a small notebook of steps for things you do often (like logging into your bank app or joining a Zoom call). You can also use your phone's Notes or Reminders app to help you remember things.

4. Keep Security Top of Mind

Stay alert to scams or suspicious messages. Trust your instincts—if something feels "off," it probably is. Don't be afraid to ask for a second opinion before clicking a link or sharing personal info.

5. Join a Learning Group

Look into local library classes, community center workshops, or online platforms like Senior Planet, GetSetUp, or even YouTube channels that explain tech step-by-step. Surrounding yourself with learners like you builds confidence and connection.

6. Celebrate Small Wins

Every time you learn something new or solve a problem, take a moment to be proud. Confidence grows with experience, and you're building a foundation that will carry you forward.

Your Digital Future Awaits

You've already done something remarkable by picking up this book, turning each page, and giving the digital world a try. The tools you've explored can help you live more independently, connect more deeply with others, and find joy in everyday things—from listening to music to seeing your grandchild's smile on a video call.

Technology doesn't have to be intimidating. It can be empowering, enriching, and even a lot of fun.

So go ahead:

- Explore a new app.

- Reach out to a loved one online.

- Try a new hobby you never imagined you'd find through your phone or tablet.

- Bookmark a site that makes your life easier or more exciting.

You don't need to become an expert overnight. You just need to stay open, stay curious, and most importantly—**keep going**.

Final Thought

The digital world is no longer just for the young—it's for everyone. And that includes **you**. So embrace the journey, ask questions, learn at your own pace, and know that the best part of technology isn't the device—it's what **you do with it**.

Here's to a brighter, more connected, and more empowered future.

You've got this!

Author's Note

From Oluchi Ike

Writing this book has been a personal journey—one inspired by the stories, questions, and quiet frustrations of many wonderful seniors I've met, both in my professional life and personal circles. I've watched brilliant minds hesitate to explore the digital world—not because of a lack of intelligence, but because of a fear of doing something "wrong," pressing the "wrong button," or simply being overwhelmed by all the noise of technology.

I want you to know: it's okay to feel that way. It's okay to feel unsure. But it's *more than okay*—it's **powerful**—to decide to try anyway.

This book was written with love, patience, and respect for you—the reader who may be stepping into unfamiliar territory, but who is choosing to grow. My goal has never been to impress you with tech jargon or long-winded explanations. Instead, I simply wanted to create a friendly, reassuring companion that guides you one step at a time toward the digital lifestyle you deserve.

Technology shouldn't leave anyone behind. It should connect us, support us, and help us thrive—at every age.

So, whether you're reading this book on a tablet, a printed copy, or as a PDF on your laptop… I just want to say **thank you**. Thank you for trusting me with your time and your learning. I hope this guide becomes a tool you can return to, share with others, and continue growing from.

Here's to curiosity, courage, and lifelong learning.

With warmest regards,

Oluchi Ike

References

1. **AARP (American Association of Retired Persons)**

   Website: https://www.aarp.org

   A trusted resource for seniors, offering tech guides, safety tips, and app recommendations.

2. **Senior Planet from AARP**

   Website: https://seniorplanet.org

   Provides free online classes and tutorials on technology and digital skills tailored for older adults.

3. **National Institute on Aging (NIA)**

   Website: https://www.nia.nih.gov

   Offers health, wellness, and tech safety resources for older adults.

4. **TechBoomers**

   Website: https://techboomers.com

   A free educational site that teaches seniors how to use popular websites and apps like Facebook, YouTube, and Amazon.

5. **Cyber Seniors**

   Website: https://cyberseniors.org

   A nonprofit organization providing digital training and mentorship for seniors.

6. **Google Safety Center**

   Website: https://safety.google

   Offers privacy tips, security tools, and how-to guides on protecting personal information online.

7. **Common Sense Media**

   Website: https://www.commonsensemedia.org

   A helpful source for evaluating online content and avoiding misinformation.

8. **Consumer Financial Protection Bureau (CFPB)**

   Website: https://www.consumerfinance.gov

   Provides safety tips on online banking, fraud prevention, and financial literacy.

9. **CDC - Healthy Aging and Technology Use**

   Website: https://www.cdc.gov/aging

   Research and tips on how older adults benefit from using technology to stay connected and healthy.

10. **Pew Research Center – Internet and Technology Reports**

    Website: https://www.pewresearch.org

    Offers data on tech usage among seniors and trends in digital adoption.

11. **Apple Support & Android Help Centers**

    o   https://support.apple.com

    o   https://support.google.com/android

        For step-by-step help with smartphones, accessibility settings, and apps.

12. **YouTube Help Center**

    Website: https://support.google.com/youtube

    A useful reference for learning to watch, subscribe to, and manage video content.

13. **Library of Congress – Digital Collections & eBooks**

    Website: https://www.loc.gov

    Offers free access to digital books, resources, and cultural content.

If You Enjoyed This Book, Try My Other Works

By Oluchi Ike

Thank you for spending time with *"Tech for Seniors: Essential Apps and Websites for a Digital Lifestyle."* I hope it empowered you to explore technology with more confidence and joy.

If you found this guide helpful, you may also enjoy my other books focused on personal growth, modern living, and lifelong learning:

Green Living: A Comprehensive Guide to Sustainable Practices

A practical, step-by-step guide to reducing waste, choosing eco-friendly products, and living sustainably in today's world.

Building a Remote Business: A Guide to Starting and Growing a Successful Remote Business

Learn how to create, manage, and scale a thriving business entirely online—perfect for freelancers, entrepreneurs, and aspiring digital nomads.

Mindfulness and Meditation for Modern Living

Discover how to bring calm and clarity into your day with simple mindfulness and meditation techniques.

The Psychology of Success: How Mindset, Habits, and Resilience Drive Achievement

Unlock the mental tools that successful people use to stay motivated, overcome obstacles, and reach their goals.

Cybersecurity for Everyday Life

A no-nonsense guide to protecting your devices, identity, and personal information in the digital age.

Stay Connected

Want to know when my next book comes out? Visit my website, follow me on social media, or join my mailing list to receive updates, bonus resources, and special offers.

Website: *Coming soon*

Email

Facebook

Instagram

www.ingramcontent.com/pod-product-compliance
Lightning Source LLC
LaVergne TN
LVHW060123070326
832902LV00019B/3107